Special Symbols:

This book is organized to guide the individual through the training. In addition to the Notes section there are a number of symbols used to help the participant throughout the presentation and workshop. For your convenience these symbols are repeated at the introduction of each section of this workbook.

Suggestion:

This symbol represents a suggestion or is a general statement relating to facilitation of the training.

Tip:

This symbol represents a tip to the Facilitator and is specific to the concept that the Facilitator is presenting.

Question:

This symbol represents a question that may be asked to the Facilitator or to the participants in the workshop. It is intended to foster interaction during the training.

Table of Contents

Section 1

Section 2

Section 3

Section 4

Section 5

Section 6

Introduction to Lean

Participant Workbook

In this Section

- Review the history of Lean & learn Lean Methodology
- Study the components of Lean
- Understand the Workshop Content

Participant Workbook Provided To:

_____

 Suggestion   **Tip**   **Question**

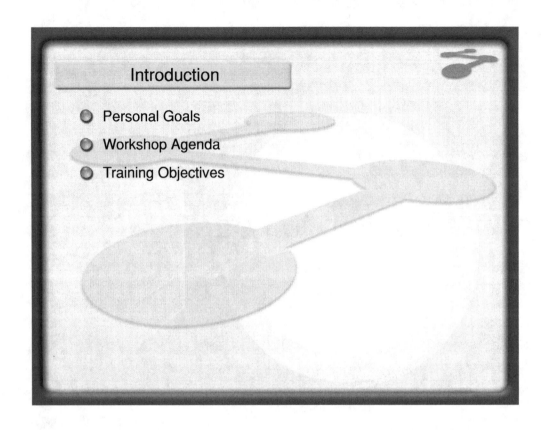

Notes, Slide 2:

_____

_____

_____

_____

_____

_____

Tip:
As you go through this presentation, remember to stay focused on the general concepts and look for what is common to your experience, not what is different.

Notes, Slide 3:

_____

_____

_____

_____

_____

_____

Tip:
To understand how Lean fits in your organization, ask the facilitator specific questions regarding the history of Lean.

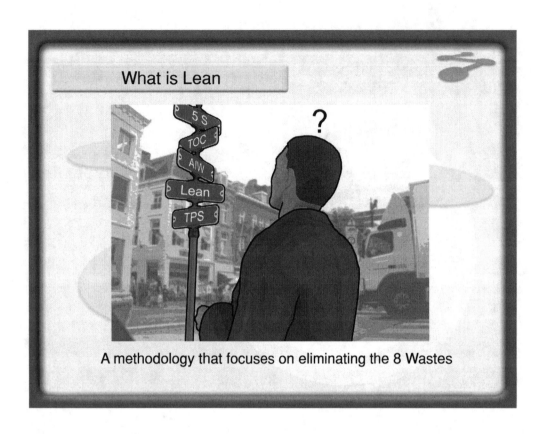

A methodology that focuses on eliminating the 8 Wastes

Notes, Slide 4:

_____

_____

_____

_____

_____

_____

Suggestion:
Be organized and pre-pared. Arrive early and be willing to engage the concepts.

Cycle Time Reduction

"One of the most noteworthy accomplishments in keeping the price of _____ products low is the gradual shortening of the production cycle. The longer an article is in the process of manufacture and the more it is moved about, the greater is its ultimate cost."

Who is being quoted here?
When was this said?

Notes, Slide 5:

_____

_____

_____

_____

_____

_____

Question:

Who is being quoted here? When was this said?

_____

_____

_____

History of Lean

- Lean's Birthplace: USA
  - 1900 est. Time & Motion Studied
  - 1913 Ford Production System established
- Lean first practiced in Japan
  - 1950's Dr. Demings Management System is studied
  - 1973 Toyota Production System
- Lean now world-wide
  - 1990's Starting in the USA
  - 2000+ Lean integrating into Corporate Strategies
    and expands beyond Manufacturing to Supply
    Chain & Logistics

Notes, Slide 6:

_____

_____

_____

_____

_____

_____

Tip:
Lean Manufacturing is a term credited to a gentleman named James P. Womack. He studied the Toyota Production System and co-authored a book entitled, "The Machine that changed the World."

Lean Supply Chain - Defined

- A Lean Supply Chain & Logistics process is streamlined to reduce and eliminate waste, or Non Value-Added activities, to the total Supply Chain flow and the products moving within the Supply Chain
- Waste can be measured in time, inventory, and unnecessary costs
- Material and Information within the Supply Chain should flow

Notes, Slide 7:

Tip:
Think of some examples in your business where material or information doesn't flow.

Supply Chain & Logistics

- Functions span across the entire Supply Chain Network
- Integrates plan, source, make, deliver, and return processes
- Includes important activities, such as:
  - Information Management
  - Purchasing
  - Inventory Flow Scheduling and Control
  - Logistics-Production Coordination
  - Order Fulfillment
  - Distribution Facilities Management
  - Transportation Systems Operation and Infrastructure
  - Customer Service

Notes, Slide 8:

_____

_____

_____

_____

_____

Tip:
The Bullwhip Effect is a series of events that leads to supplier demand variability up the Supply Chain. Trigger events include frequency of orders, varying quantities ordered, or the combination of both events by downstream partners in a Supply Chain. As the orders make their way upstream, the perceived demand is amplified and produces what is known as the bullwhip effect.

Costs vs. Sales

Typical Supply Chain & Logistics costs as a percent of Sales:

- Logistics: 7-8%
- Supply Chain: 50-70%

For every $1 saved through the Supply Chain you would need to have an additional $3-$10 of Sales in order to equal the same contribution

Notes, Slide 9:

Lead Time Reduction

- Quality & Time
  - Cost & Time
    - Delivery & Time
      - Safety & Time
        - Morale & Time

- QCDSM

Notes, Slide 10:

Tip:
For an operation to be successful we need to focus on the use of time in all respects. It is the only resource that we cannot get more of, and for this reason focusing on time will provide the best motivation for all other factors that are important to business.

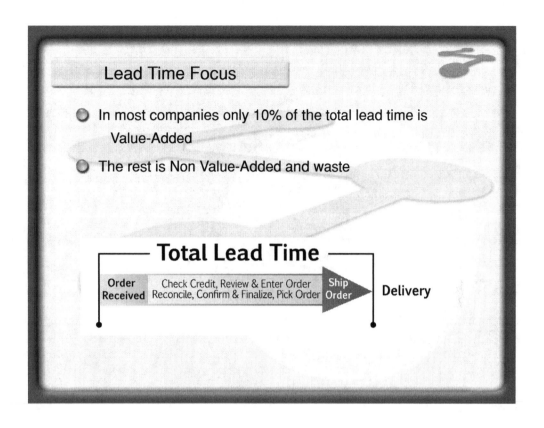

Notes, Slide 11:

_____

_____

_____

_____

_____

_____

_____

Suggestion:
Ask questions when you feel clarification is needed.

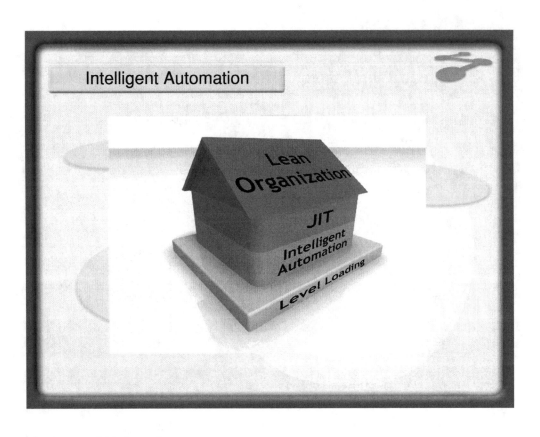

Notes, Slide 12:

_____

_____

_____

_____

_____

_____

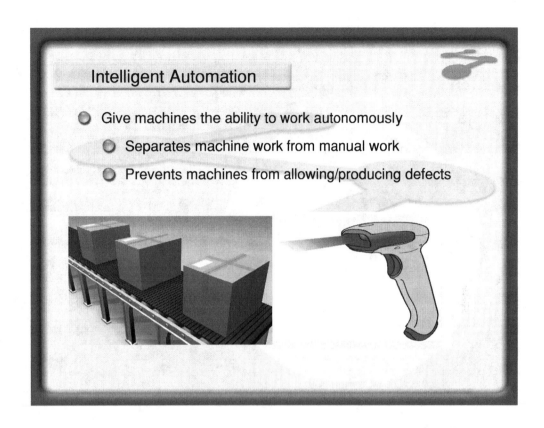

Intelligent Automation

- Give machines the ability to work autonomously
- Separates machine work from manual work
- Prevents machines from allowing/producing defects

Notes, Slide 13:

_____

_____

_____

_____

_____

_____

Tip:
Automating something does not mean that it is autonomous. For example, a car has automation components, but it is not autonomous to you needing to drive the vehicle.

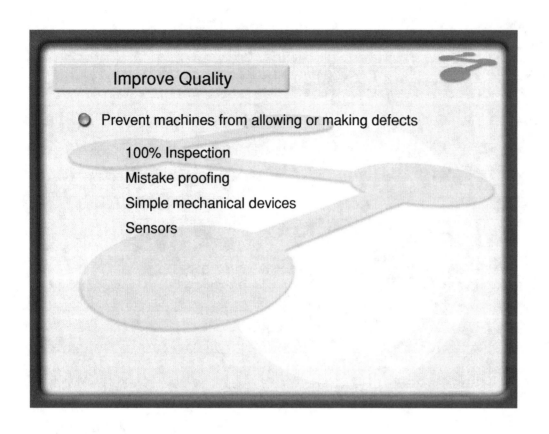

Improve Quality

- Prevent machines from allowing or making defects

  100% Inspection

  Mistake proofing

  Simple mechanical devices

  Sensors

Notes, Slide 14:

_____

_____

_____

_____

_____

_____

Tip:
Think of intelligent automation as making many small steps towards the machine performing some tasks without supervision.

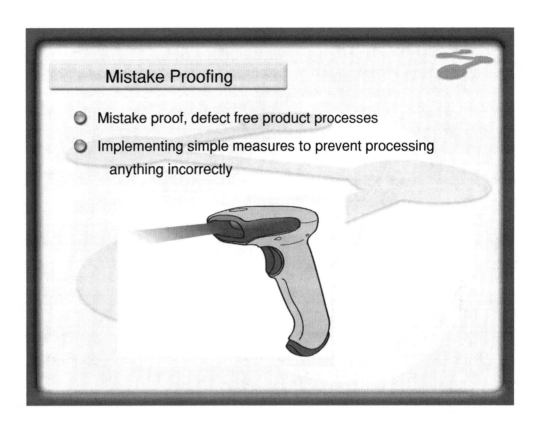

Notes, Slide 15:

Tip:

Think of a way to stop a machine or person from having the option of making a defect. This is the ultimate goal of mistake proofing.

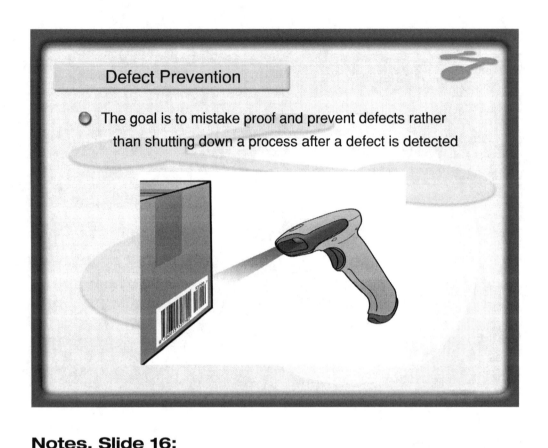

Defect Prevention

- The goal is to mistake proof and prevent defects rather than shutting down a process after a defect is detected

Notes, Slide 16:

_____

_____

_____

_____

_____

_____

Tip:
As this illustration shows, there may be an easy way to prevent a defect from occurring.

Question:

Is there an example of this in your area?

_____

_____

_____

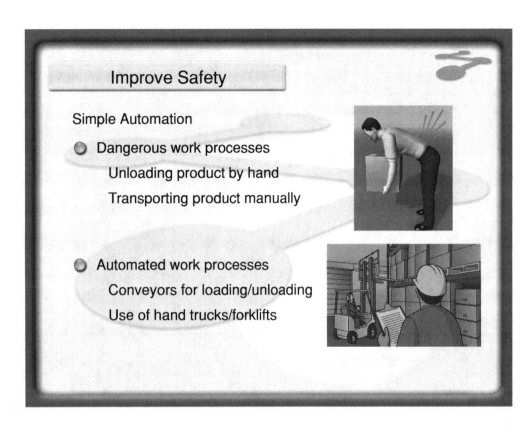

Notes, Slide 17:

_____

_____

_____

_____

_____

_____

Suggestion:

Think of ways to improve safety without having to spend too much money. This will allow the process of improving, in itself, to be flexible to change.

Supply Chain & Logistics

Participant Workbook

In this Section

- Learn the differences between Lean and Traditional processes
- Benefits of Lean
- Steps to Building Lean
- How to Measure Lean

 Suggestion   **Tip**   **Question**

Traditional vs. Lean

Characteristic	Traditional Supply Chain & Logistics	Lean Supply Chain & Logistics
Scheduling	Forecast - Push	Customer Order - Pull
Replenishment	Stock	Customer Order
Lead Time	Long	Short
Lot Size	Large - Batch & Queue	Small - Continuous Flow
Inspection	Sampling - by Inspectors	100% - at source by workers
Layout	Functional	Product Flow
Empowerment	Low	High
Inventory Turns	Low	High
Flexibility	Low	High
Cost of Goods Sold	High & Rising	Lower & Decreasing

Notes, Slide 19:

_____

_____

_____

_____

_____

Suggestion:

Think of where your own company is in terms of Lean for each of the characteristics listed. Are you under the Lean Supply Chain & Logistics or does your company still operate under traditional processes?

Benefits

- Lower Supply Chain costs
- Faster turnaround and lead times
- Fewer errors
- Ongoing cost reduction and service improvement culture
- Process standardization throughout the company

Notes, Slide 20:

_____

_____

_____

_____

_____

_____

Steps for Building Lean

- Develop a Lean culture of team-based Continuous Improvement, reducing less functional "silo" thinking

- Understand value from the customer's perspective

- Value Stream Map critical Supply Chain processes and identify wastes and places where material/information doesn't "flow"

- Determine core competencies; find partners with complementary abilities

Notes, Slide 21:

Tip:
While these steps may seem logical and fairly straight forward, understand that it is a long journey of transformation and there will be bumps along the way, especially in terms of cultural change.

Steps for Building Lean

- Benchmark Best Practices; use that information to set goals for Kaizen Events
- Create flow, visibility, and flexibility in the Supply Chain VSM "Future State"
- Continually measure performance

LEAN

Continually Measure

Flow, Visibility

Benchmark

Notes, Slide 22:

_____

_____

_____

_____

_____

_____

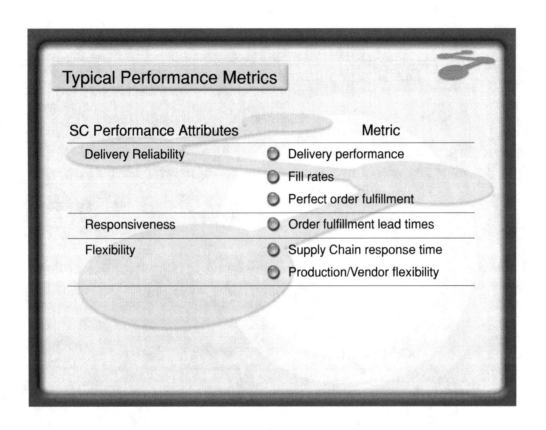

Typical Performance Metrics

SC Performance Attributes	Metric
Delivery Reliability	Delivery performance
	Fill rates
	Perfect order fulfillment
Responsiveness	Order fulfillment lead times
Flexibility	Supply Chain response time
	Production/Vendor flexibility

Notes, Slide 23:

Suggestion:

Ask the facilitator to discuss and demonstrate actual metrics that have been used in real companies.

Typical Performance Metrics

SC Performance Attributes	Metric
Costs	Cost of goods sold
	Total SC management costs
	Value-Added productivity
	Warranty/Returns processing costs
Asset Management Efficiency	Cash-to-cash Cycle Time
	Inventory days of supply
	Asset turns

Notes, Slide 24:

_____

_____

_____

_____

_____

_____

Understanding the 8 Wastes

Participant Workbook

In this Section

- Lean Supply Chain & Logistics and the 8 Wastes
- Understanding the 8 Wastes
- Study the components of Lean
- Understand the Workshop Content

 Suggestion   **Tip**    **Question**

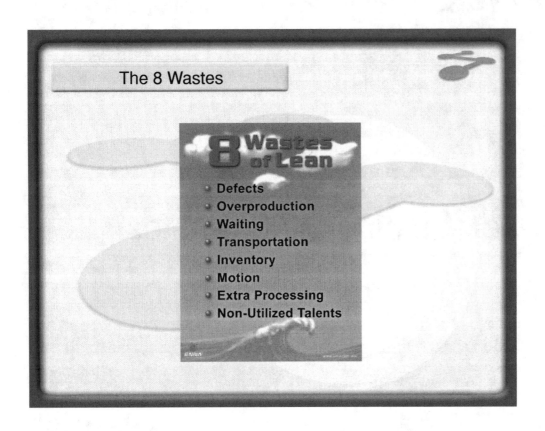

Notes, Slide 26:

_____

_____

_____

_____

_____

_____

Tip:

The 8 Wastes are a fundamental building block of Lean. Ask the facilitator to fully explain the wastes so that you understand them completely.

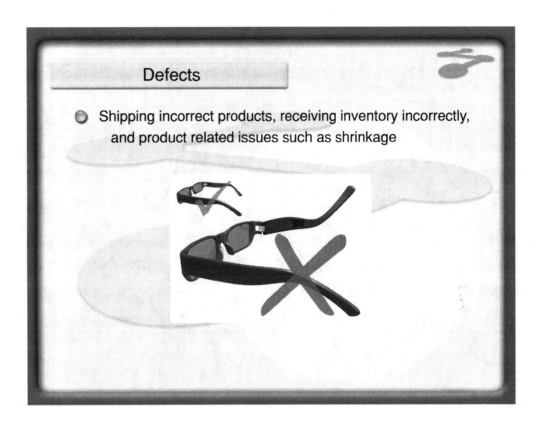

Notes, Slide 27:

_____

_____

_____

_____

Waste Definition: _____

_____

Additional Example: _____

_____

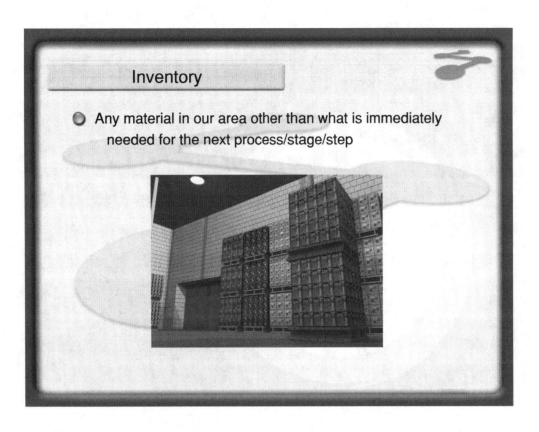

Inventory

- Any material in our area other than what is immediately needed for the next process/stage/step

Notes, Slide 28:

_____

_____

_____

_____

Waste Definition: _____

_____

Additional Example: _____

_____

Question:

What are the three stages that inventory lives as in your company?

_____

_____

_____

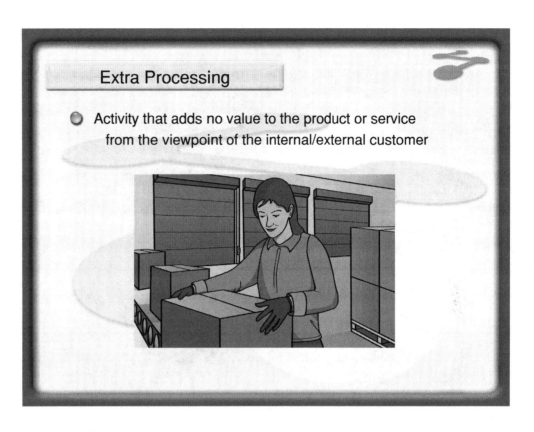

Notes, Slide 29:

_____

_____

_____

_____

_____

Tip:

This is the hardest
waste to find, however
the solution is simple.
If you think about it,
if it is truly a waste of
processing then the ulti-
mate solution is to find
a way to not do it.

Waste Definition: _____

_____

Additional Example: _____

_____

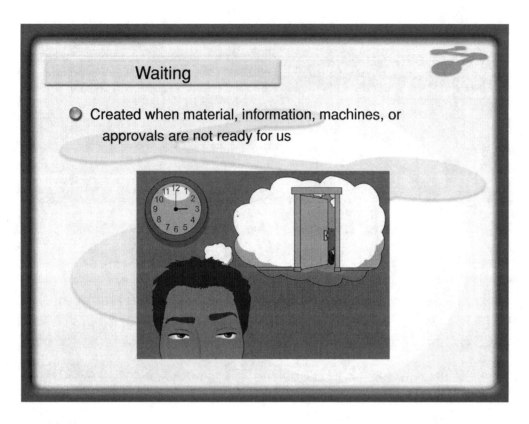

Notes, Slide 30:

_____

_____

_____

_____

Waste Definition: _____

_____

Additional Example: _____

_____

Suggestion:
Try purposely waiting for someone or something rather than doing something. It is hard to wait.

Question:

What are some times that you have waited, or when do you wait and what do you wait for?

_____

_____

_____

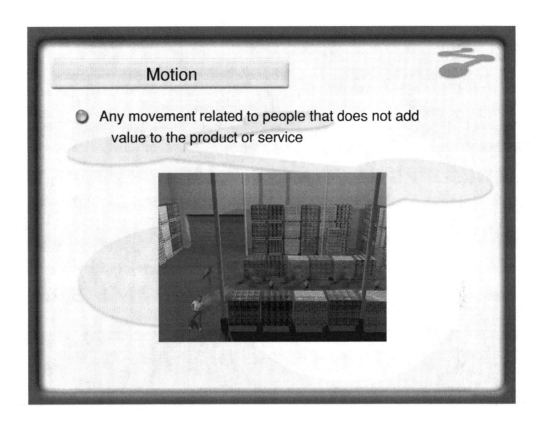

Motion

○ Any movement related to people that does not add value to the product or service

Notes, Slide 31:

_____

_____

_____

_____

Waste Definition: _____

_____

Additional Example: _____

_____

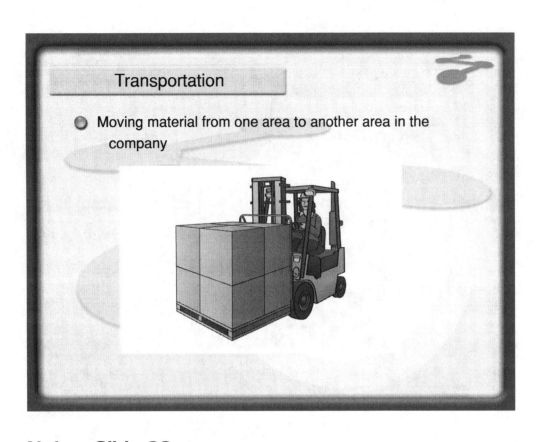

Transportation

- Moving material from one area to another area in the company

Notes, Slide 32:

_____

_____

_____

_____

Waste Definition: _____

_____

Additional Example: _____

_____

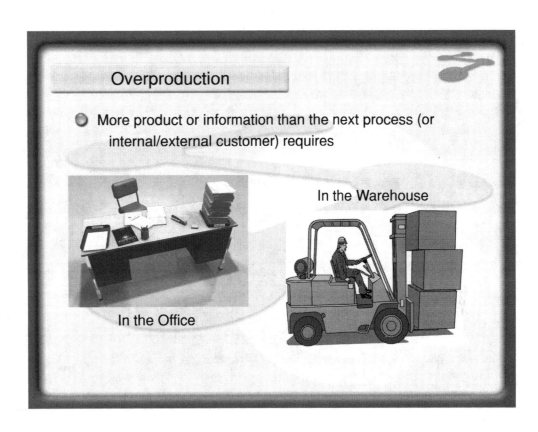

Overproduction

- More product or information than the next process (or internal/external customer) requires

In the Warehouse

In the Office

Notes, Slide 33:

_____

_____

_____

_____

_____

Tip:
Operations should look at ways to only produce what is truly needed. Anything more will result in loss of efficiency and effectiveness.

Waste Definition: _____

_____

Additional Example: _____

_____

Question:
Why do you think we give overproduction such a high score?

_____

_____

_____

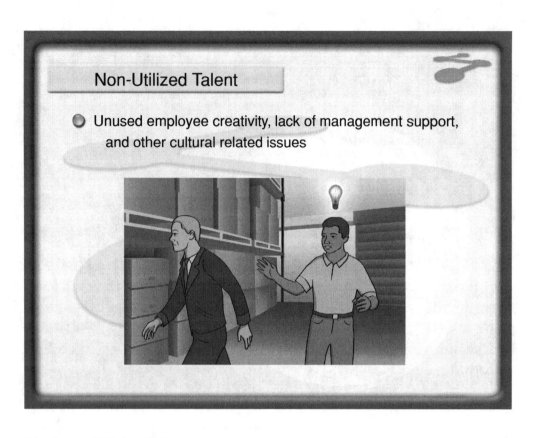

Notes, Slide 34:

_____

_____

_____

_____

Waste Definition: _____

_____

Additional Example: _____

_____

Components

Function	Areas to look for Waste & Continuous Improvement
Lean Distribution	Data entry, transportation and motion, inventory control, shipment of products and inventory levels, distribution network optimization
Lean Transportation	Core carrier programs, transportation administrative processes and automated functions, mode selection and pooling of orders, combining of multi-stop truckloads, "right sizing" equipment, import/export transportation processes, inbound transportation, and backhauls

Notes, Slide 35:

Tip:
Try to think of areas within your company that are wasteful. Think in terms of jobs functions that affect later, downstream processes. Do data entry errors create more or less errors downstream?

Components Cont'd.

Function	Areas to look for Waste & Continuous Improvement
Lean Procurement	Partnering and collaborating with suppliers, supplier visibility, Vendor Managed Inventory (VMI) programs, joint reviews
Lean Suppliers	Lean review and assessment of suppliers, Lean transformation of suppliers
Lean Customers	Customer requirements, Point of Sale (POS) and inventory data, best practices from Lean customers

Notes, Slide 36:

_____

_____

_____

_____

_____

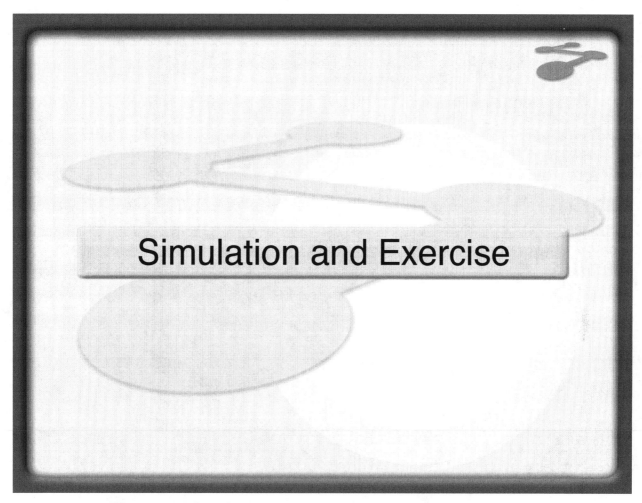

Simulation and Exercise

Participant Workbook

In this Section

- A guide to Flow Simulation

 Suggestion   **Tip**   **Question**

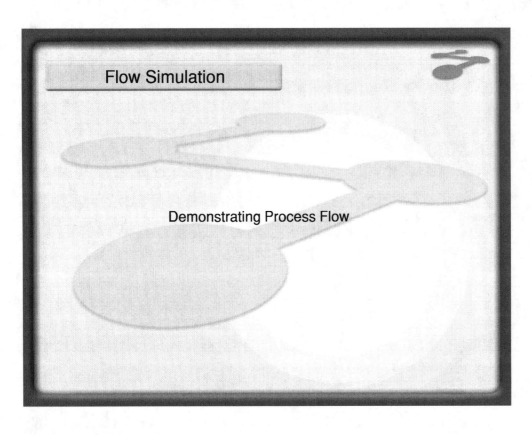

Notes, Slide 38:

_____

_____

_____

_____

_____

_____

Notes, Slide 39:

_____

_____

_____

_____

_____

_____

Avro Business Overview

○ Operating Policies

Keep batches together with paper clips

Batch size of 6 planes

Consistent pace at assigned operations

Inventory control: FIFO

Shift	6 minutes
Lead Time Goal	2 minutes (special order entered @ 2 minutes into shift)
Sales Price	3 million per unit
Customer Demand	35 planes per shift
Inventory	Raw issued, WIP, Finished Goods
Inventory Cost	Valued at 1 million per issued material
Profit	Sales - ((Labor + O/H) + Inventory Cost)

Notes, Slide 40:

_____

_____

_____

_____

_____

_____

Tip:
Although each participant will have a specific task, also consider how the inventory is moving from one process to the next process.

Production Schedule

- Production Batch
  - Batch of 6 airplanes per SKU

- Special Order
  - Detailing a special colored star on a wingtip

- Changeover (Setup)
  - After every 6 airplanes, fold setup paper one time (except for Op10)

Notes, Slide 41:

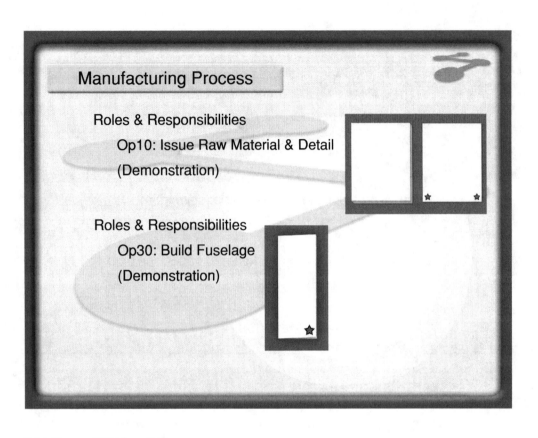

Notes, Slide 42:

_____

_____

_____

_____

_____

_____

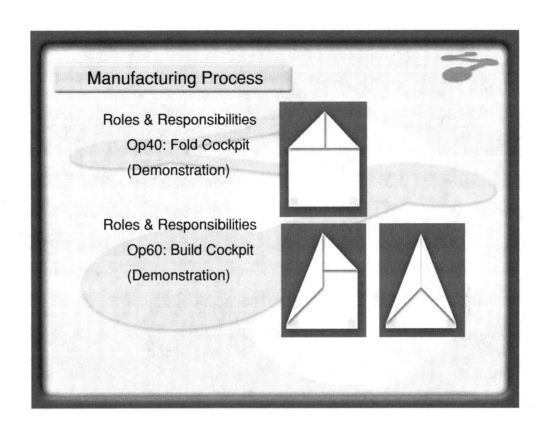

Notes, Slide 43:

_____

_____

_____

_____

_____

_____

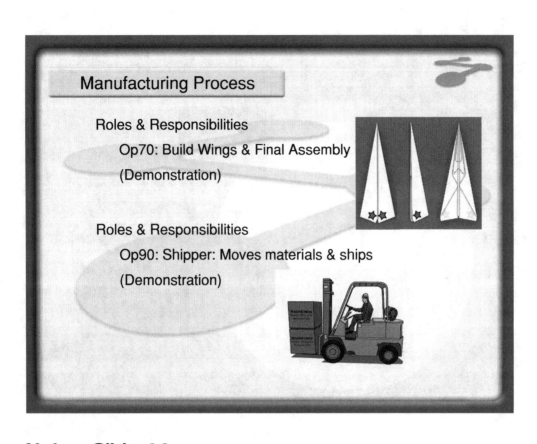

Notes, Slide 44:

_____

_____

_____

_____

_____

_____

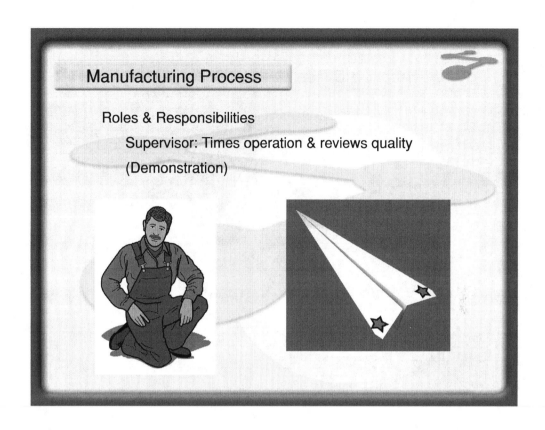

Manufacturing Process

Roles & Responsibilities

Supervisor: Times operation & reviews quality

(Demonstration)

Notes, Slide 45:

_____

_____

_____

_____

_____

_____

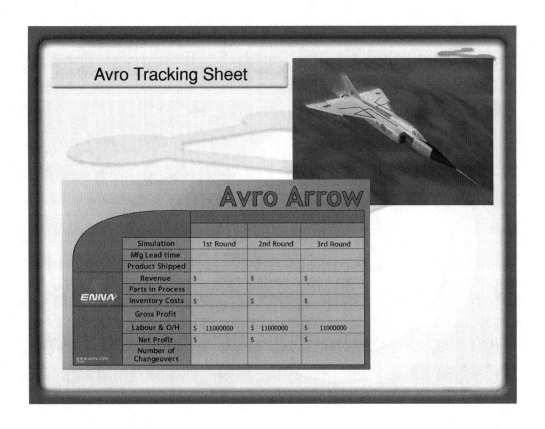

Notes, Slide 46:

_____

_____

_____

_____

_____

Question:

What observations did you make during the different stages of the simulation?

_____

_____

_____

Simulation

Simulation	1st Round	2nd Round	3rd Round
Mfg Lead time			
Product Shipped			
Revenue	$	$	$
Parts in Process			
Inventory Costs	$	$	$
Gross Profit			
Labour & O/H	$ 11000000	$ 11000000	$ 11000000
Net Profit	$	$	$
Number of Changeovers			

Avro Arrow

ENNA

www.enna.com

Advanced Lean Tools

Participant Workbook

In this Section

- Learn Advanced Lean Tools such as Just In Time, Takt Time, and Flow
- Benefits of Level Loading
- How to Measure Takt Time

 Suggestion   **Tip**    **Question**

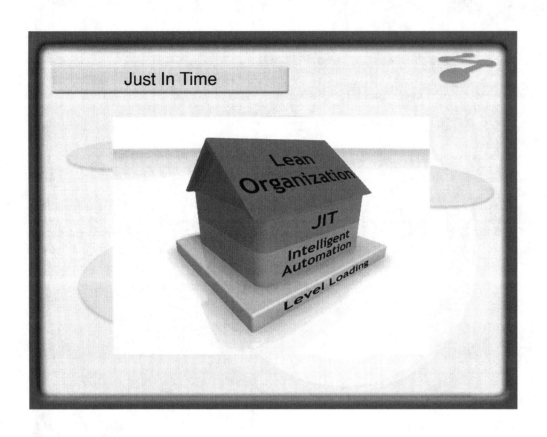

Notes, Slide 48:

_____

_____

_____

_____

_____

_____

Just In Time

- Having what the customer needs, when they need it, where they need it, in the quantity needed
- Uses the least amount of effort, materials, equipment, machinery, and space to get the job done
- Exposes hidden problems and the 8 Wastes
- Just In Time is three principles:
  - Takt Time
  - Flow Production
  - Pull System

Notes, Slide 49:

_____

_____

_____

_____

_____

_____

Tip:

JIT focuses on what the next customer in the process needs. If you are satisfying your next customer in your company then you are doing the right thing.

Takt Time

- The word "Takt" is German for the baton that an orchestra conductor uses to regulate the timing of a musical piece

- In business, Takt Time is the "Beat Time" for operations set by the customer; it is the rate at which the customer buys products

- Takt Time cannot be measured; Takt Time is only calculated

Notes, Slide 50:

_____

_____

_____

_____

_____

Question:

What does Takt Time in operations stand for?

_____

_____

_____

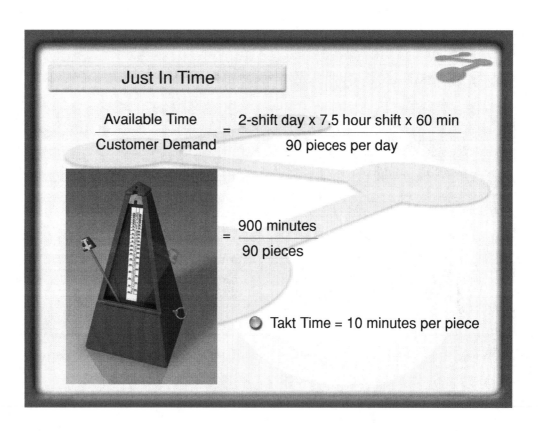

Notes, Slide 51:

_____

_____

_____

_____

_____

_____

Tip:
One key concept in Lean or JIT is the end result of the equation of Takt Time. It is minutes per piece, not pieces per minute. This is the fundamental difference to calculating operations.

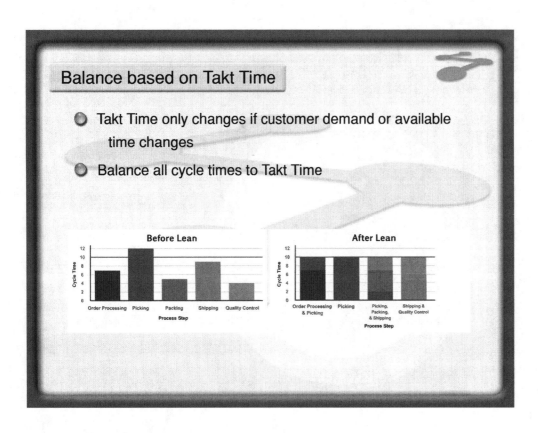

Notes, Slide 52:

_____

_____

_____

_____

_____

_____

Question:

What are some of the benefits for balancing to Takt Time?

_____

_____

_____

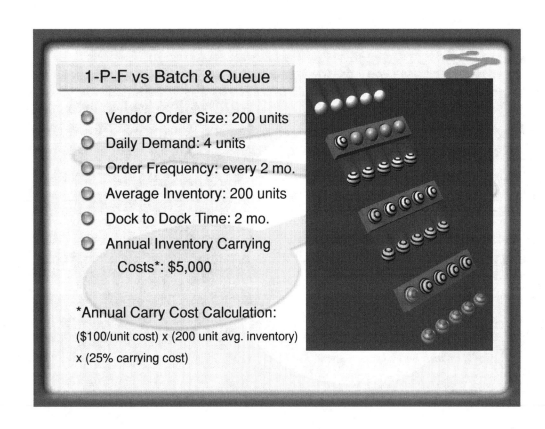

1-P-F vs Batch & Queue

- Vendor Order Size: 200 units
- Daily Demand: 4 units
- Order Frequency: every 2 mo.
- Average Inventory: 200 units
- Dock to Dock Time: 2 mo.
- Annual Inventory Carrying Costs*: $5,000

*Annual Carry Cost Calculation:

($100/unit cost) x (200 unit avg. inventory)

x (25% carrying cost)

Notes, Slide 53:

Suggestion:

Ask the Facilitator to explain this concept, as it is key to understanding the impact of batching on the cost of operations.

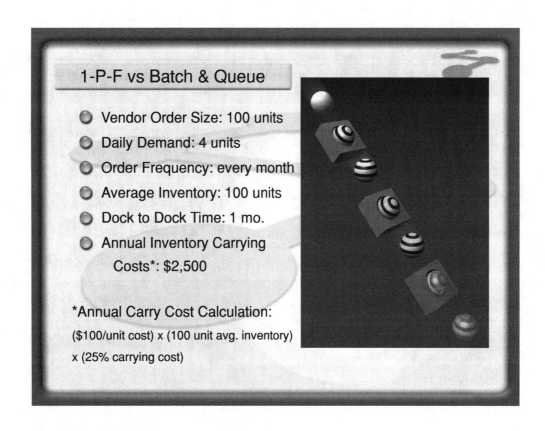

1-P-F vs Batch & Queue

- Vendor Order Size: 100 units
- Daily Demand: 4 units
- Order Frequency: every month
- Average Inventory: 100 units
- Dock to Dock Time: 1 mo.
- Annual Inventory Carrying
  Costs*: $2,500

*Annual Carry Cost Calculation:

($100/unit cost) x (100 unit avg. inventory)

x (25% carrying cost)

Notes, Slide 54:

Tip:

Notice that the change in these processes are the amount of inventory in process, the size of the staging areas, and the transportation between each stage. By going to a Lean operation, you can minimize those kinds of costs.

1-P-F Defined

- Moving product from one process to the next without waiting
  - Quality: Bad products are immediately apparent
  - Cost: Less Work-In-Process and space needed
  - Delivery: Shortest lead time
  - Safety: Less motion
  - Morale: Problems revealed sooner

Notes, Slide 55:

_____

_____

_____

_____

_____

_____

Question:

What are other benefits of One-Piece-Flow?

_____

_____

_____

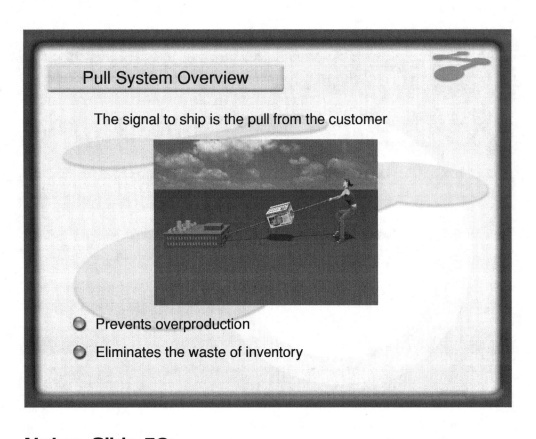

Notes, Slide 56:

_____

_____

_____

_____

_____

_____

Question:

What are the two kinds of customers for a company?

_____

_____

_____

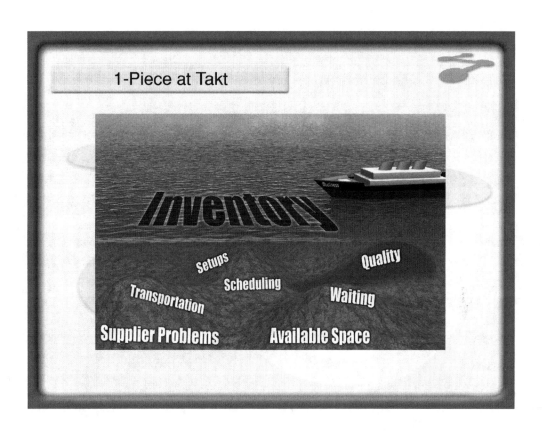

1-Piece at Takt

Inventory

Setups
Scheduling
Quality
Transportation
Waiting
Supplier Problems
Available Space

Notes, Slide 57:

Suggestion:
Engage the trainer on concepts that seem to be counter intuitive.

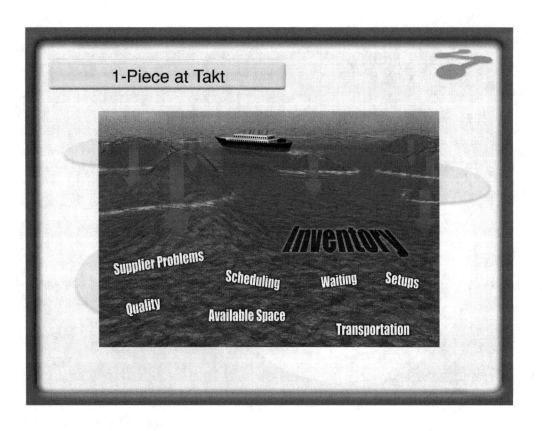

Notes, Slide 58:

_____

_____

_____

_____

_____

Question:

What rock in your department should be looked at first?

_____

_____

_____

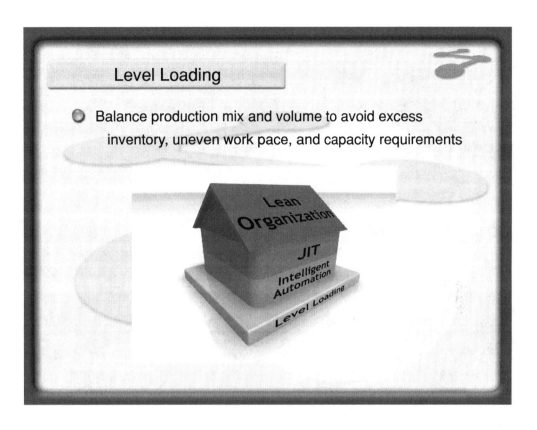

Level Loading

- Balance production mix and volume to avoid excess inventory, uneven work pace, and capacity requirements

Notes, Slide 59:

_____

_____

_____

_____

_____

_____

Level Loading

Examples in Warehouse Operations

- Adapting pocessing rates to variation in customer demand
    - Variation in volume
    - Variation in product mix
    - Maintain constant staffing
    - Minimize travel time
    - Maximize productivity

- Leveling allows for processing a variety of products smoothly throughout each day, week, and month

Notes, Slide 60:

Tip:
Level loading provides the motivation to reduce a number of activities, such as assembly time, setup time, and order entry time.

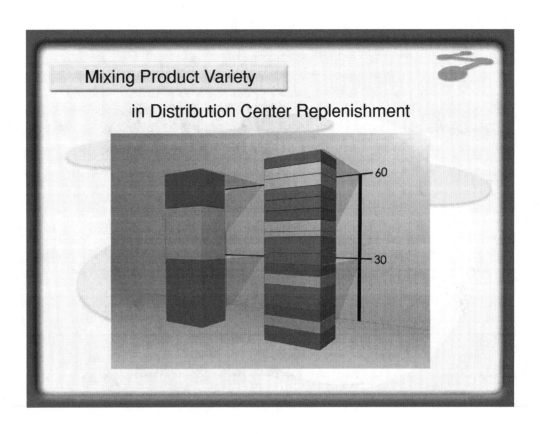

Notes, Slide 61:

_____

_____

_____

_____

_____

_____

Question:

Can you see any other benefit to the goal of producing in smaller batches?

_____

_____

_____

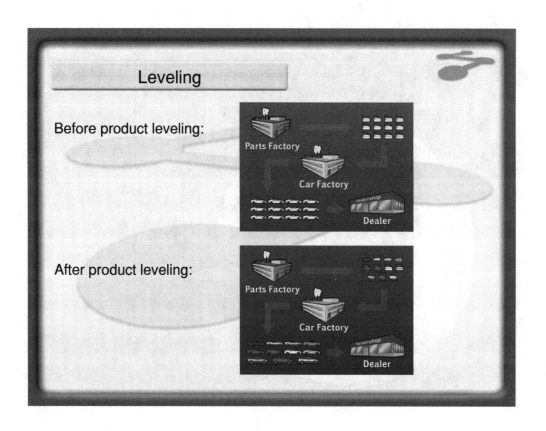

Notes, Slide 62:

_____

_____

_____

_____

_____

_____

Question:

What are the advantages of this type of system?

_____

_____

_____

Level Loading Benefits

Throughout the Supply Chain

- Less Work-In-Process inventory
- Processing is agile to customer demands
- More consistent work due to variety in production or processing
- Less fluctuation in capacity requirements
- Less Finished Goods inventory
- Avoids creating excess Finished Goods inventory

Notes, Slide 63:

_____

_____

_____

_____

_____

_____

Suggestion:

Take a few minutes to write down any comments, conclusions, or concepts that you have learned during this section of the presentation.

Conclusions:

_____

_____

_____

_____

Simulation Round 3

Participant Workbook

In this Section

- Final round of the Simulation
- 8 Wastes Observation Exercise

 Suggestion   **Tip**   **Question**

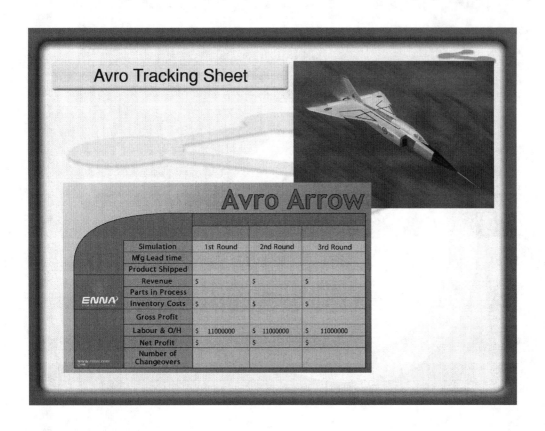

Notes, Slide 65:

_____

_____

_____

_____

_____

_____

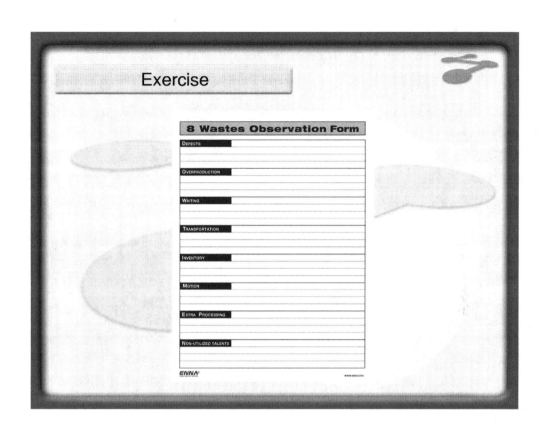

Notes, Slide 66:

Tip:
For this exercise, work in teams of two people to discuss your observations.

Introduction to Lean Supply Chain Assessment

Facilitator: _____   Name: _____

Workshop: _____   Date: _____

Circle or write the answer that best fits the question or completes the statement.

1. _____ **What company started what is now known as Lean?**
   a) Toyota
   b) Volvo
   c) General Motors

2. _____ **What is the first element in JIT?**
   a) Takt
   b) Flow
   c) Pull

3. _____ **Of the 8 Wastes which one is the worst?**
   a) Motion
   b) Inventory
   c) Overproduction

4. _____ **Which of the following illustrates an activity that does *not* add value?**
   a) ordering parts from a supplier
   b) accumulating parts in front of the next worker
   c) delivering product to the customer

5. _____ **VSM stands for_____.**
   a) Valuable Service Measure
   b) Value Stream Mapping
   c) Value, Service, Morals

6. _____ **In business, Takt Time is _____.**
   a) the amount of time it takes to make something
   b) the pace of customer demand
   c) total time for products to go through the facility

7. _____ **Vendor Managed Inventory is a form of _____.**
   a) Outsourcing
   b) A "push" system
   c) Economies of scale

8. _____ **Which of these is not a benefit of Level Loading?**
   a) Less inventory
   b) Agile processing to meet customer demand
   c) Reduced flow

9. _____ **In a Pull-based system, who signals production?**
   a) VP of Operations
   b) Production Manager
   c) Customer

10. _____ **Benefits of a Lean Supply Chain include _____.**
    a) longer lead times
    b) fewer errors
    c) less standardization

11. _____ **Level Loading allows production of _____ each day, week, and month.**
    a) a variety of products smoothly throughout
    b) few product varieties throughout
    c) large products with few variety throughout

12. _____ **Supply Chain & Logistics costs as a percent of sales are typically in the range of _____.**
    a) 40-60%
    b) 60-70%
    c) 10-20%

13. _____ **What is the definition of a Flow production system in business terms?**
    a) Everyone adds value when they want
    b) Moving the product from one process to the next without waiting
    c) Inventory will move from one place to the next and wait to be worked on

14. _____ **Level Loading your operation will make it much easier to _____.**
    a) make batches of materials
    b) minimize WIP inventory, less finished goods, and avoid fluctuations in capacity
    c) maximize WIP inventory, produce more finished goods, and increase fluctuations in capacity

1:a, 2:a, 3:c, 4:b, 5:b, 6:b, 7:a, 8:c, 9:c, 10:b, 11:a, 12:b, 13:b, 14:b